Winning Futsal

Secrets to Success in the Youth Game

By Rob Bell

ISBN-10: 0692477446

ISBN-13: 9780692477441

Cover Design by Rob Bell
Illustrations by Rob Bell

Dedication

To my wife, kids, and parents. Their love of futsal has enabled mine. A sincere thank you to Joey Almeida, Jamil Tahir, Kevin Crow, and Doug Murray for their vision, encouragement and knowledge. Finally, a huge debt of gratitude to every player I've ever been lucky enough to coach. The learning went both ways.

Table of Contents

Futsal in America – soccer will never be the same

Many big soccer countries are scared about our new pro futsal league. They worry if America gets organized on the futsal side, it will lead to world domination on the soccer side. – Keith Tozer, USMNT Coach

We've heard all the excuses of why U.S. soccer lags the top nations in the world. Pay to play, video games, too many other sports, lack of a soccer culture, etc. It goes on and on. In Spain they pondered the same question a few decades back. Other questions perplexed them as well. Why did the Brazilians play so sensationally? Why did they dribble, pass, and *think* so differently? Was it the Samba, beach soccer, or the weather?

The Spanish eventually concluded it was futsal. Brazilians have played more futsal in the past 80 years than any other country. And what do Pelé, Zico, Socrates, Ronaldo, Ronaldinho, and Neymar have to say about the sport? They all agree futsal was *essential* in their path to stardom.

Spain now has fully integrated futsal into their soccer curriculum, and the 2010 FIFA World Cup trophy is a nice bit of evidence to confirm the obvious: futsal matters hugely in the technical and tactical development of youth. Angel Maria Villar Llona, the president of the Spanish Federation, has publicly stated that futsal was a major reason for Spain's World Cup victory.

Bulldogs Fútsal Club – humble, stumble & Eureka!

"Success is not a good teacher, failure makes you humble."
– Shahrukh Kahn

Humble

In 2010, I was recently divorced and was lucky to have $200 in the bank at month's end. I had started dating again and was embarrassed that fast food burritos were the high end of the dining scale. So when my charismatic principal, Jamal Fields, asked the staff to start after school clubs, I ran with it. I envisioned the extra pay allowing for Thai noodles and mango smoothies on a white tablecloth. And so out of a dining crisis, Bulldogs Fútsal Club was born.

And a humble birth it was. Cracked asphalt, beat up utility cones, and worn PE hockey goals were all I could offer the kids as we trained just outside the glow of our gym where basketball had dibs. That first winter I ran three trainings per week with 30 students attending each. I reasoned it was just a novelty and soon the attendance would dip. Instead the attendance increased. It was all very rewarding, but I quickly grew frustrated with the lack of equipment and poor facilities.

As a kid on summer vacations in Bolivia, I marveled at the futsal courts that dotted the city of Santa Cruz. Everywhere you looked kids were playing "fulbito" on these basketball-sized courts. I always dreamed of having similar courts to play on here in the States. Would it be possible to raise the money and build one at Junction Ave K-8 School?

The answer was yes. Within three months we had raised over $35,000 through a series of grants and league fees. Our new Saturday futsal league was a hit with over 160 students signing up. A few months later, we built two courts on site. They are the first of their kind on a school campus in the U.S.

SANTA CRUZ, BOLIVIA

LIVERMORE, CALIFORNIA

Stumble

A group of boys soon stood out for their playing abilities. With all the chest puffing that comes from a new league and facilities, I entered this group into a local futsal tournament. Surely we would hold our own. In our three games, the only thing we held was the exit door. We lost by over a combined 75 goals. It got so bad the scorekeeper stopped tracking the opponent's goals past 20. We were outplayed, out-coached, and out-organized. It was a unique humiliation that still stings years later. However, it was a *first step*.

The next day almost every player stopped by my classroom with the question, "When's the next tournament?" I was stunned. Didn't they want to give up after the weekend's thrashing? Just the opposite! So we started training 3x a week and entering local tournaments whenever possible. We also played a number of scrimmages against local competitive soccer teams. Most of our team was comprised of players whose families could not afford organized soccer. So I had a captured audience that was eager to learn. I poured myself into books, YouTube, and pestered local coaches for knowledge.

Eureka!

Several months of futsal only training led to stunning results. The boys were now routinely thumping the area's top soccer teams by 20+ goals in scrimmages. One astute visiting coach, Doug Murray, of Ballistic United Soccer Club, made the connection: futsal was gold for technical and tactical development. The Bulldogs players showed superior ball control and off-the-ball movements. They attacked and defended relentlessly. Something special was going on.

Soon thereafter I joined BUSC as their first Director of Futsal and BUFC (Ballistic United Futsal Club) was founded. Kevin Crow, BUSC's Club Director and former USMNT player described the new futsal club as "a club within a club." A number of Bulldogs boys joined BUSC as well. We focused on training the club's youngest players, and in March of 2015, Ballistic "Bulldogs" United Futsal Club won two age groups at the United States Futsal Federation's Northwest Regional Championship held in San Jose, California. A few months later at USFF's National Championship held in Anaheim, CA, our u8 and u9 teams again repeated as champions. In our first major competitions, we were hauling off silverware. We were the only club to win multiple championships at both events. The week following Nationals, a number of our players attended a futsal camp hosted by USA Futsal and FC Barcelona. At week's end, Andreu Plaza, the youth director of futsal at FCB, invited six BUFC players to train at La Masia.

2015 USFF NORTHWEST REGIONAL CHAMPIONS - U8 & U9

2015 USFF NATIONAL CHAMPIONS – U8 & U9

The following ideas will hopefully increase the learning curve for you and your players. Wins and losses are meaningless concepts when not grounded in better ones like sportsmanship, respect, and good manners. Hopefully all learning will be filtered through these themes. Good luck with your futsal journey. You are one of the lucky few to be called Futsal Coach. *¡Suerte!*

Developing Technique – do you have sole?

> ➤ *Receiving, shielding, dribbling, passing, shooting*

"Happiness resides not in possessions, and not in gold, happiness dwells in the soul." - Democritus

Receiving

The heart of futsal is ball control. Dribbling on a hard, flat surface quickly reveals a player's technique, usually within seconds. You can either master the ball, or you can't. The sole of the foot is an invaluable tool. Besides helping on the dribble, it is essential for *receiving* the ball. It offers immediate control on a fast surface. Toes up and a heel down leads to an instant ball stop.

Shielding

To protect the ball from an aggressive defender, shielding or protecting the ball is necessary. The ball is controlled with the back foot while the front foot stays between the defender and the ball. The player on the ball should extend a bent arm to hold the defender off. Players are encouraged to bend the knees for balance, keep the head up for vision, and maintain the ball moving so as to not provide an easy target for the defender. Entering a shield is easy enough, but *exiting* one is a different deal. We teach our players two methods:

Double Shield – while dragging the ball with the sole, the player spins to their "blind" side. The "double" part of this motion refers to the arms. The initial bent arm gives way to the player's second arm that now wards off the defender in the spin motion.

Fake and Go – the player quickly drags the ball back with the sole as if moving to the blind side only to then push the ball forward with the instep to the open "vision" side.

Dribbling

The following "Big 4" are essential dribbles.

*1) **Sole-Control*** - the ball is rolled diagonally with the sole of the foot and controlled with the instep of the other.

2) *Iniesta* - the ball is moved with the inside of the feet from one foot to the other in an "L" shape. This is Iniesta's signature move.

*3) **Pull-push out** - the ball is stopped, pulled back with the sole, and then pushed out with the instep. This "V" shape movement often avoids a defender's stab.*

4) ***Dime stop*** - the ball is pushed diagonally with the outside of the foot and then stopped "on a dime" with the sole of the same foot. Next the dribbler changes direction by pushing with the outside of the opposite foot.

Only four dribbles are taught? No. Others are taught, but these four are deemed essential. Once mastered, the court becomes a playground.

Passing

Accuracy: since there is no grass to slow the ball, precision passing is necessary. Providing a leading pass is rare. Most often passing is *to feet*. The demand to be precise leads to improved accuracy.

Weight: with many defenders inside a condensed area, futsal often requires firm passes to maintain possession. Softer struck balls allow defenders opportunities to intercept.

Shooting

The **toe poke** is synonymous with futsal. In Brazil 2014 we witnessed a number of goals from South American teams that involved this finishing technique. From my own South American travel experience (over a dozen trips), futsal is played considerably more than soccer. You are what you play, and so with Brazil and Argentina leading the way, innumerable players of quality have emerged. Pelé, Socrates, Zico, Maradona, Ronaldo, Ronaldinho, Messi, and Neymar all swear by futsal. And how about that "other" Ronaldo from Portugal? Well, Cristiano says futsal **is** the reason for his spectacular technique.

Ok, back to the toe poke. Times are a changing, but here is the U.S. in some circles, the toe poke is still much maligned. Kids are told to "use the laces" for power. All well and fine, but the addition of the toe poke to the toolbox is simply a no brainer. All parts of the foot should be mastered for dribbling, passing, and *finishing*. Would you limit a carpenter to only a bucket of nails and a hammer, and *hide* the power drill?

Toe poke: most often used when the shooter's shoulders are squared to the goal. The kick allows for a shorter windup and more powerful blast since the toe area is a harder, more fortified part of the shoe. The ball is released quicker than a normal shot, so keepers are often caught unaware.

Movement off the ball – I move therefore I am (a futsaler)

> ➤ *Checking, 1-2's, and back post finishing*

> *"I like to move it move it. I like to move it move it."*
> - King Julian in Madagascar

Just like Holmes & Watson, Romeo & Juliet, or In-N-Out Burger & a freeway, *Futsal & Movement* go together. You simply can't have one without the other.

Why the emphasis on movement? Simply put, a moving player is tough to track while a stationary player is easy to defend. Movement is a must for every advanced offense. This is not unique to futsal or soccer: think of the Golden State Warriors' swirling offense. Concluding that movement is critical is the easy part. Putting it into practice is where things get tricky . . . until now.

Checking

A team is only as good as its checks. Spacing, timing, and quickness all come into play. When building up from one's own half, checking is mostly the domain of the 7 & 11 "forward" positions in our 2-2 formation. They create space by taking their defenders past the midcourt line and then checking back to the 2 & 5 positions.

When deep inside the opponent's half on a kick-in, the opposite is true. With the 7 or 11 kicking-in, the 2 & 5 are now expected to check to the ball much as they would on a corner kick.

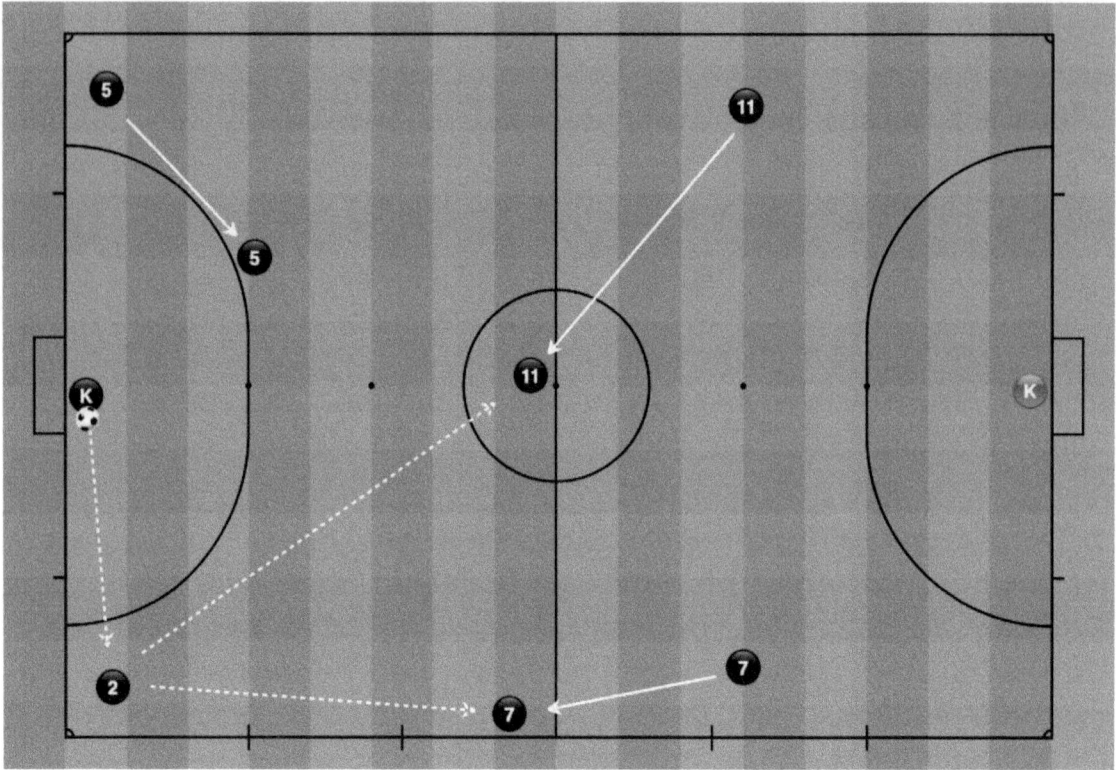

7 & 11 CHECKS

1-2's, wall passes, & give-&-goes

All mean the same thing: the ability to play a quick two player passing combination. The initial player passes, moves to space, and then receives the ball back from the second player. It's that simple, except it's not. It is rare to see a competitive soccer or futsal team in the U.S. play consistent pass and move ball. It is at the heart of the iconic FC Barcelona style of play, yet so few can replicate it.

The 2-2 formation allows for 1-2's between the 2 & 7, and the 5 & 11. Our mantra during our training drills is "kick straight, run diagonal." It's that simple if you insist on it. The flip side of this mantra is "kick diagonal, run straight."

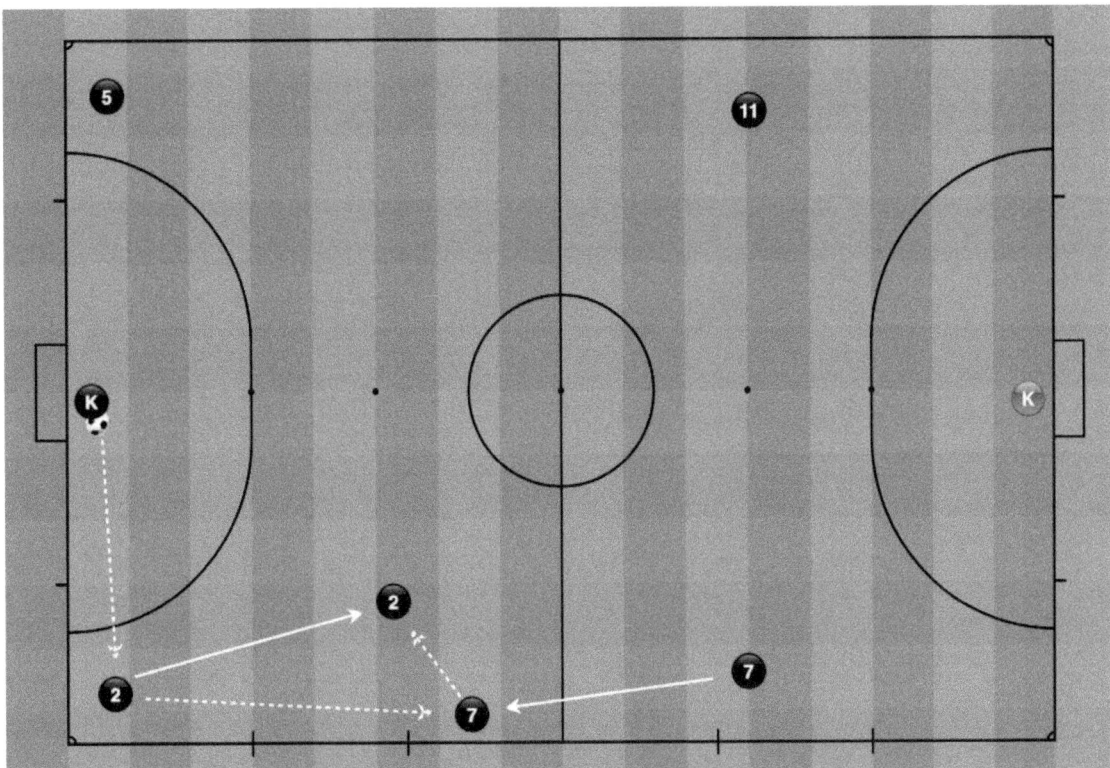

CLASSIC 1-2

Back post finishing

"Everyone wants to go to heaven, but nobody wants to die." – Peter Tosh

And everyone wants to score a goal, but not everyone wants to run like a madman to the back post. Some of the easiest goals in futsal come from back post tap-ins on the counter attack. One player possesses the ball wide in the attacking half (strong side) while another teammate dashes to the back post from the opposite side (weak side). The opponent's keeper must commit to the strong side attacker and limit the scoring opportunity at the near post. This now exposes a huge scoring window at the back post area where the weak side teammate now awaits his tap-in goal. Of course none of this comes to pass if the weak side teammate does not make the effort to *run.*

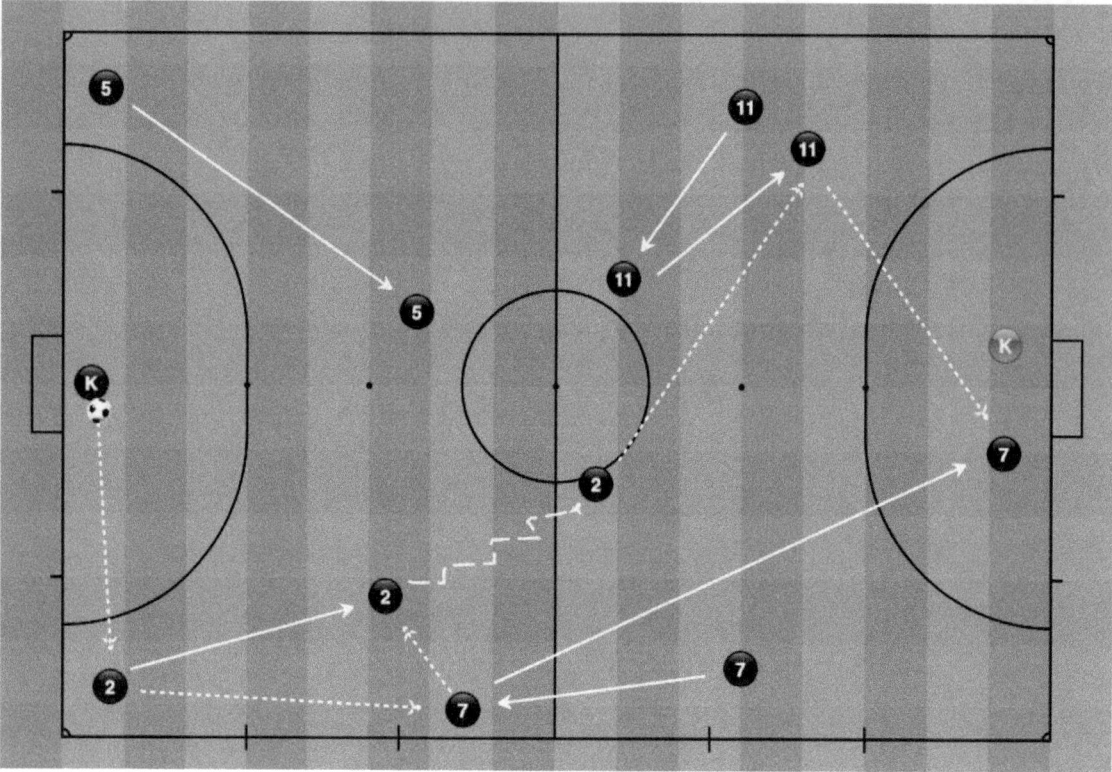

BACK POST GLORY

Build Up - attack from the back

> ➤ *1-2's, attacking the middle, and a propeller spins*

"Nobody ever defended anything successfully, there is only attack and attack and attack some more." – George S. Patton

The beauty of futsal is that labels of defender and forward are heaved out the window. In reality our 2 & 5 "defender" positions play more like soccer 10's. They are the creative forces that regulate the game. The positions are constantly required to make quality decisions on whether to dribble or pass.

Our players are free to make their own decisions; however, we do provide some guidelines and structure.

1-2's & attacking the middle

Situation: The ball is in the Keeper's hand and the 2 & 5 are deep in their corners away from the defense allowing for time and space once the ball is received. The Keeper rolls the ball to the 2.

An opponent will now quickly attack the 2. The 2 now decides if a 1-2 wall pass with the checking 7 is doable. If not doable, (perhaps the defender has the line covered) our 2 then looks to beat the opponent with a dribble to the middle. If the 2 beats this initial defender on the dribble, this will set up a 3v2 situation around midcourt. A successful 1-2 wall pass between the 2 & 7 also puts us at a numerical advantage as defenders are left behind. This is the name of the game: *beat* the initial defender through a pass or dribble and a 2v1 or 3v2 will result.

a propeller spins . . .

In addition to the 1-2 wall pass or dribble to the middle, we also have a *propeller* to spin. This possession-based tactic involves all four court players acting as *one*. In the above scenario, if the 2 decides a 1-2 with the 7 is not doable, and a dribble to a congested middle is not appropriate, then the propeller spins to life.

Words will not do the propeller justice, but here it goes: the 2 squares the ball across the court to the 5. The 2 then sprints diagonally to the middle. The 5 has the option of passing to the 11 up the line or the 2 now in the middle, *or* again squaring the ball across the court to the 7 who has now dropped into the 2's original starting point.

These two independent propellers or rotations allow for possession and an unbalancing of the defense. As the defense shifts from side-to-side, inevitable passing lanes open up and the attack begins.

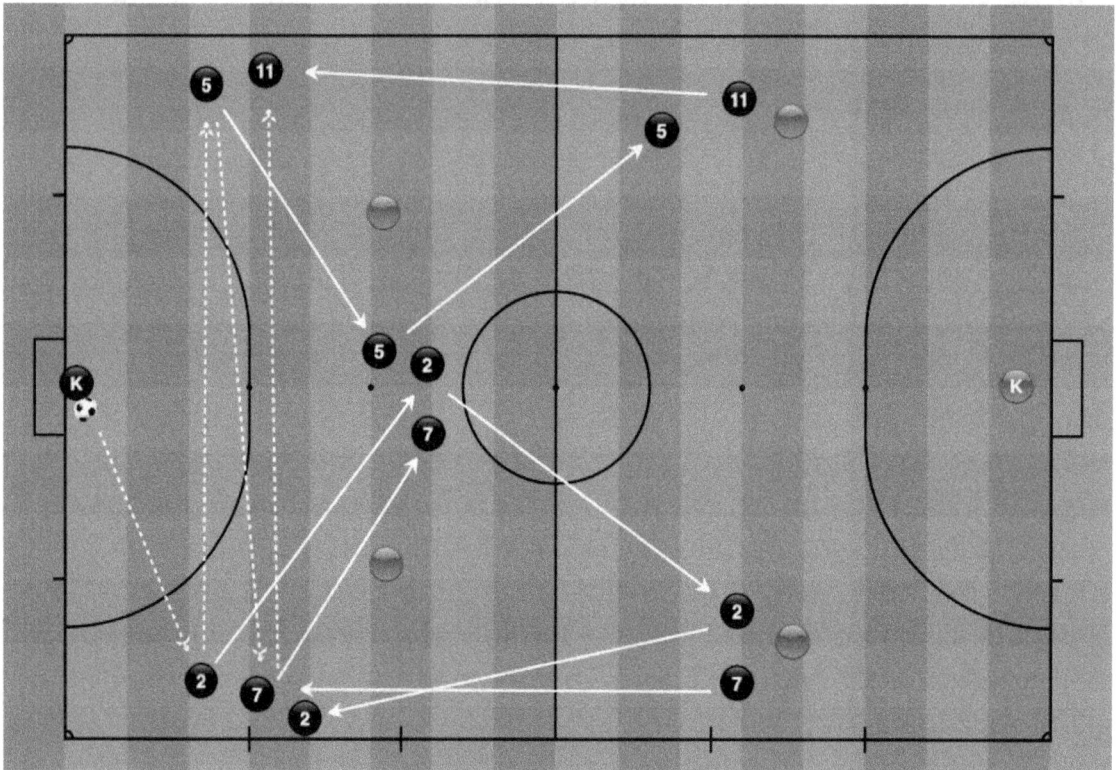

PROPELLER ROTATIONS

Keeper Play - futsal's essential position

> ➢ *Technique, Keeper Quarterback, Keeper Sweeper, Goalie Guard*

In my teams, the goalie is the first attacker, and the striker the first defender. – Johan Cruyff

In futsal no position is as critical as keeper. In addition to being the last line of defense, it is also the first point of attack. For possession purposes, the position is an essential link as well. Because of futsal's small playing area, the ball is constantly out of play. These dead ball situations involve the keeper every time. Reading the defense and making good decisions is at the heart of quality keeper play. Let's break it down.

Technique – 4 positions

In futsal the keeper has four basic ways to stop the ball. Each depends on where and how hard the ball is stuck. The keeper should always be on the balls of their feet and actively reading the game. Most professionals go gloveless to better their grip and distribution. At the youth level gloves are common, but I recommend the thinnest possible to again facilitate distribution.

The main difference between keeper play in futsal and soccer is the use of the legs to defend. In soccer, keepers are encouraged to dive and use their hands as a first option. In futsal, shots often come hard, low, and from close proximity. This requires dynamic leg play.

Situation #1 – The ball rolls to the keeper at a slow or moderate pace. The keeper now kneels and turns slightly sideways. The keeper's trailing leg comes close to touching the ground at the knee, but not quite. The knee must not touch the ground. This way the keeper can stand up quickly and distribute or chase a ball he has not properly handled. This trailing leg is pinched in to not allow a *nutmeg* possibility. The keeper captures the ball with both hands facing downward.

Situation #2 – The ball arrives at the keeper waist level or higher with force. The keeper is encouraged to deflect the ball with their hands wide or out of play. Diving for the ball may be required, but if the keeper is good with their footwork, they will often remain on their feet. Catching a forcefully struck ball is difficult especially from close range and often leads to dangerous fumbles and poaching opportunities.

Situation #3 – The ball arrives hard and low. The keeper is encouraged to use their leg to stop this type of shot. The positioning resembles that of a sprawled hockey goalie. One foot is fully extended sideways and parallel with the surface, and the other is bent backwards at the knee. Again the shot arrives with such force there is little time to get low with a hand-save, so the legs are necessary.

Situation #4 – The keeper finds himself 1v1 on a breakaway. He quickly sprints out to narrow the angle and then kneels in the position described in #1 except now the arms are extended straight outward and to the side with the hands open. This position seeks to cover the four areas the shot may go: lower left, lower right, upper left, upper right. Again the keeper should not lower their knee to the ground in case they need to quickly stand and chase the opponent if a dribble around is attempted.

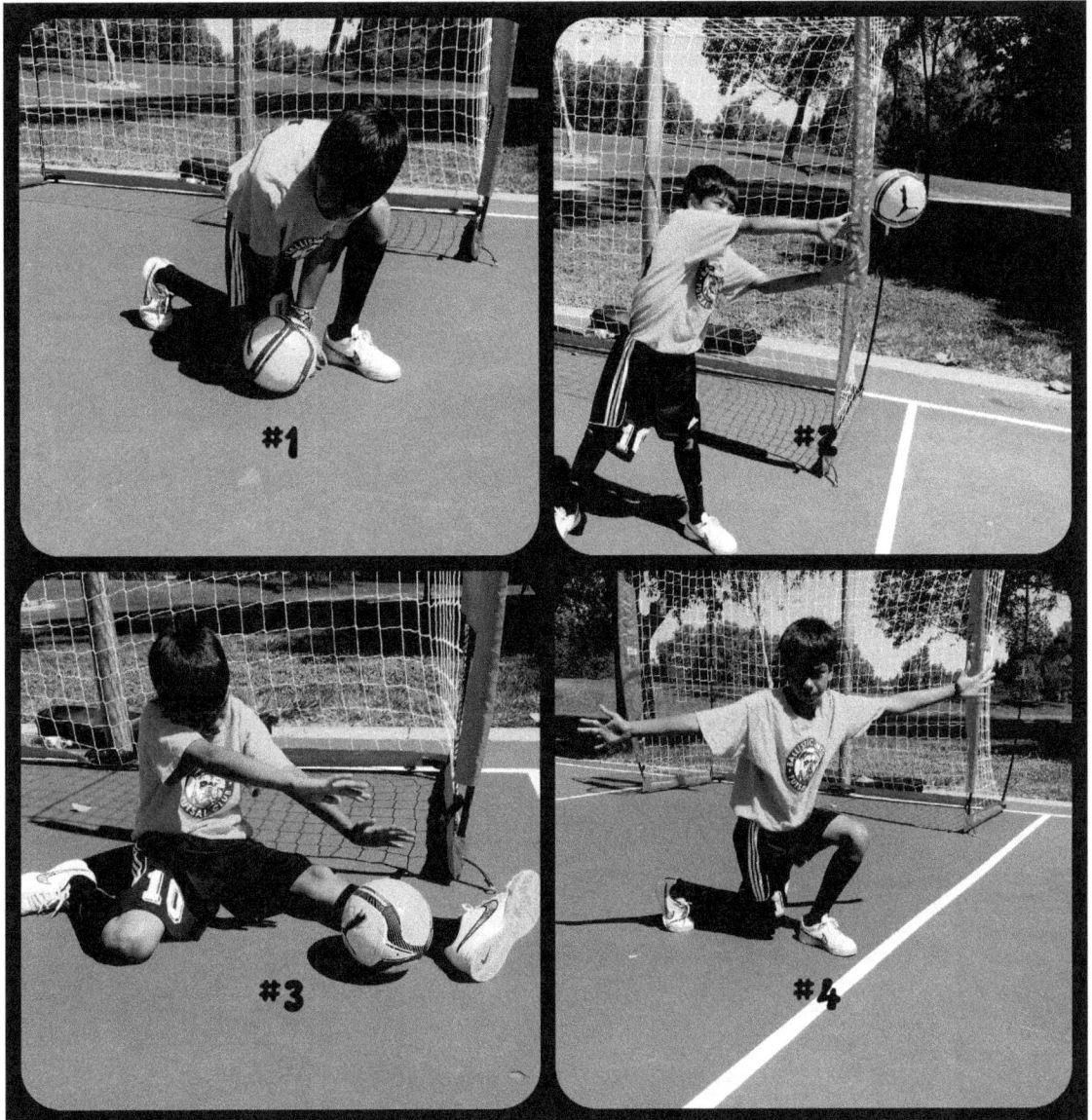

FOUR GOAL STOPPING POSITIONS

Keeper Quarterback – throw-ins

Situation #1 – The ball rolls out of bounds over the end line. The Keeper now must throw/roll the ball into play within 4 seconds – Defense plays (typical) 2-2 zone.

In our 2-2 offensive formation the 2 & 5 "defender" positions sprint to the back corners while the 7 & 11 "forwards" *stretch* up-court past the midcourt line. Possession is the name of the game at this point. Unless the 7 & 11 are wide open, we want our Keepers to safely roll the ball to the 2 or 5.

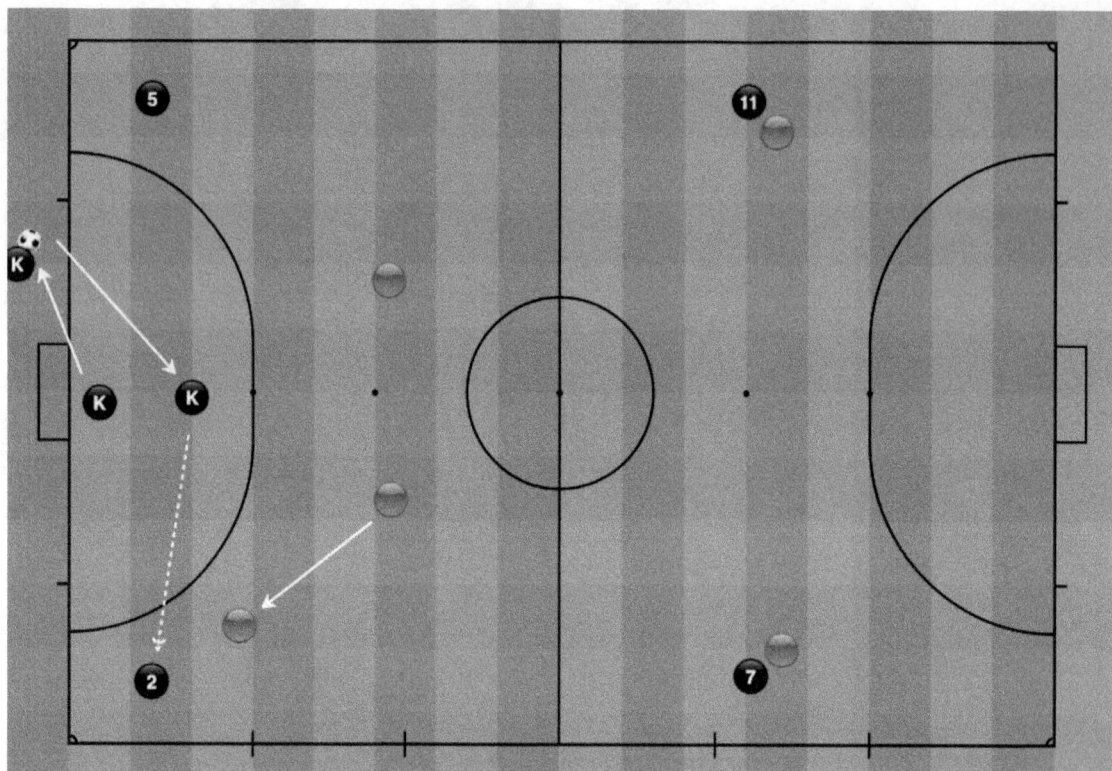

SAFE ROLL INITIATES BUILD UP

Situation #2 – Keeper must throw/roll the ball into play within 4 seconds – Defense plays man-to-man.

Our 2 & 5 are still back in their corners, and the 7 & 11 are still stretched up-court. However, it is no longer easy/safe to roll the ball to the 2 or 5 due to the aggressive man-to-man marking. In this scenario the 7 or 11 checks back to the Keeper. *But which one?* We don't want both the 7 & 11 to check into the same area. The "forward" position that checks back to the keeper is the one that is ***diagonal*** from where the ball exited over the end line. If the ball exits to the Keeper's left, then the 7 checks back. If to his right, then the 11 checks back.

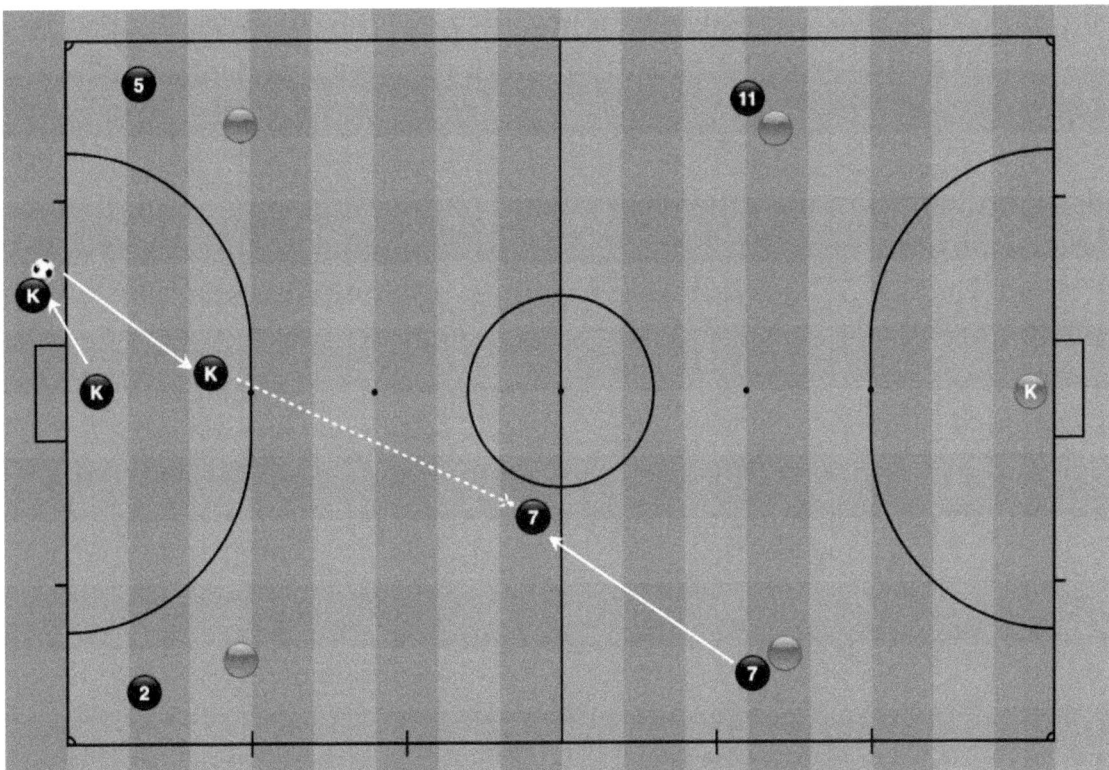

HIGH PRESS LEAVES MIDDLE OPEN

Keeper Sweeper – kick-ins – maintaining 100% possession

Ideally when the ball is over the touchline, it is quickly kicked-in to catch the defense unaware, but in most instances this isn't the case. The ball has rolled a distance away, and the defense has time to regroup. Under these circumstances, we look to retain possession with a safe re-entry pass.

From kick-ins, we should maintain possession 100% of the time. If the 7 & 11 are not open, then the Keeper may be played every time. We do not want to force a ball to the 7 & 11 and create a 50/50 scenario. The *Keeper option* allows us to maintain possession, always.

Situation #1 – The ball rolls out of bounds over the sideline. The ball is in our half and is being kicked-in by either the 2 or 5. Defense plays 2-2 zone.

The 2 or 5 looks to pass the ball forward to the checking 7 or 11. If neither position is clearly open, then the in-bounder plays back to the Keeper. The 2 & 5 must *immediately* drop down their respective sidelines to provide a safe passing angle for the Keeper.

Once the Keeper possesses the ball, he has 4 seconds to **A)** return the ball to the in-bounder **B)** switch the ball to other side of the court or **C)** dribble/pass to the middle of the court.

OPTION A

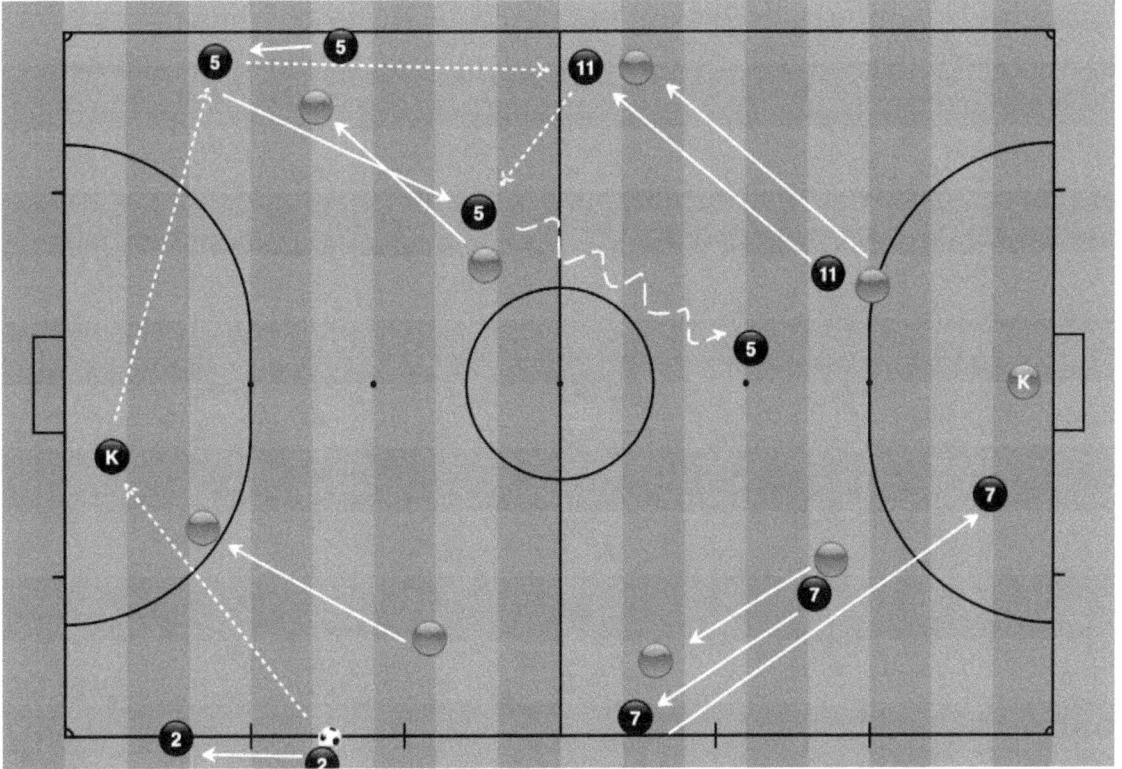

OPTION B

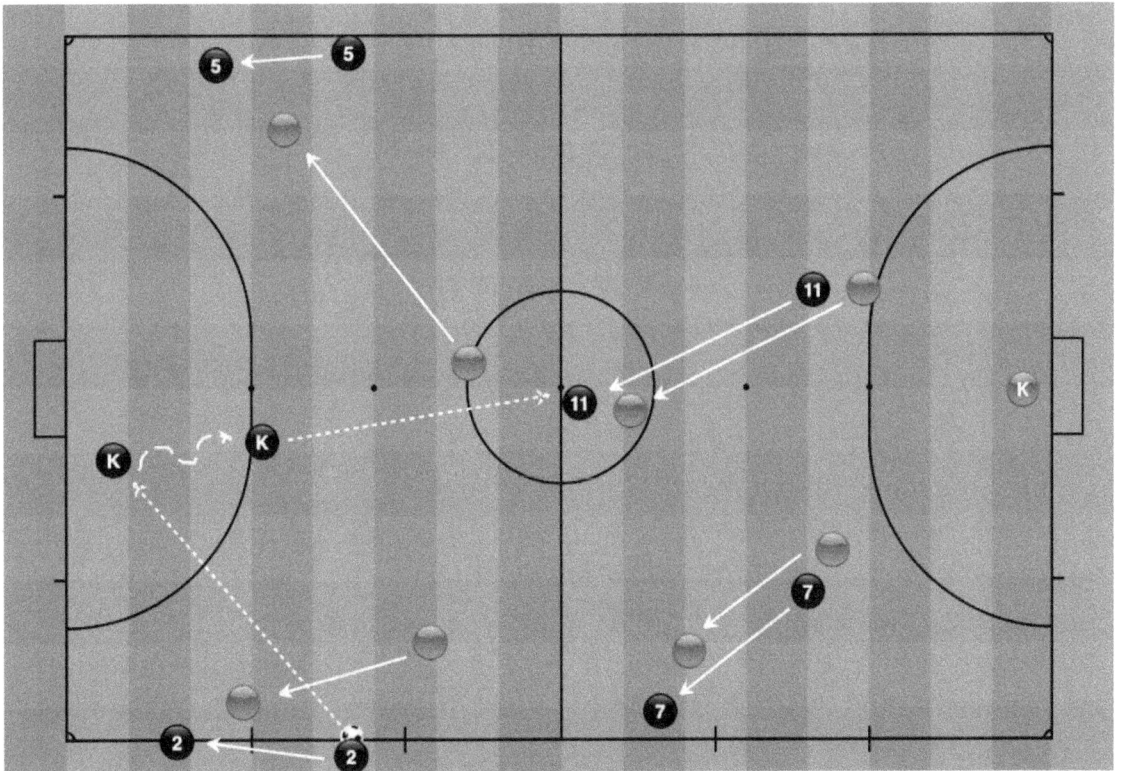

OPTION C

31

Situation #2 – The ball rolls out of bounds over the sideline. The ball is in opponent's half and is being kicked in by either the 2 or 5. Defense plays 2-2 zone.

The 2 or 5 now may use our Keeper who stands near midcourt as the first option to then blast on goal. Keeper may also pass along the A, B, C options listed above.

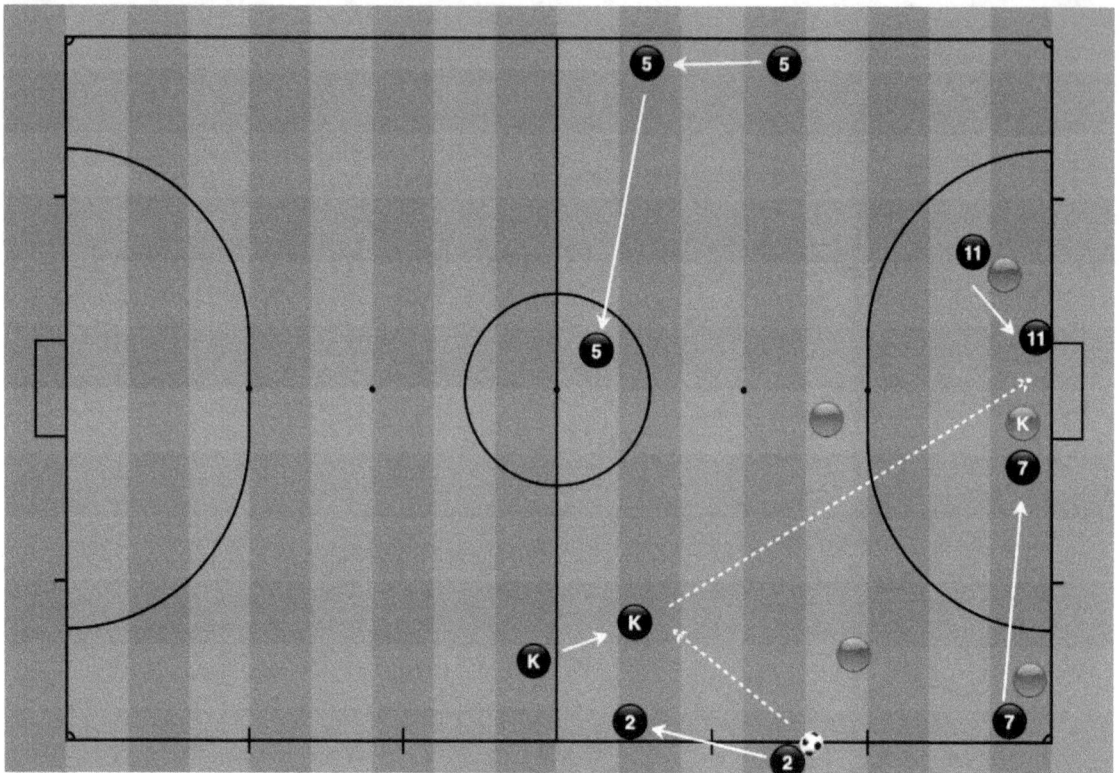

KEEPER BLAST

Goalie (Point) Guard – fast breaking

Like the Golden State Warriors' Stephen Curry, the Keeper may find the opportunity to lead a sudden *fast break* counter attack. This occurs when he catches the ball from live play and realizes the middle two defenders are split wide or behind the play. The Keeper now looks to immediately *put it down* and dribble like the proverbial bat out of hell until a defender steps up. At this point our Keeper passes (*dishes*) wide to the 7 or 11 position and retreats quickly back to goal. These bursts up the middle almost always result in placing the defense in a vulnerable 3v2 situation.

KEEPER COUNTER

Corners – a shot every time

> ➤ *positioning, checks, timing, & passing weight*

"Still around the corner there may wait, a new road or a secret gate."
– J.R.R. Tolkien

If executed properly, corner kicks should produce a shot on goal every time. We look to kick-in the ball as quickly as possible to prevent the defense from setting up. Players must immediately read the situation and line up in their positions. A corner is a set piece. And set pieces mean *goal scoring* opportunities.

Positioning – Squarish

If the 7 is on the ball, then the 2 will be on the sideline just before the midline. The 11 will be at the back post, and the 5 will be in front of the middle circle.

Checks – quick and decisive

In the above scenario, the 2 checks straight down the line. He times his run to provide the best "shooting window" between defenders. He shoots back post, so the 11 can redirect an errant shot on goal if necessary.

The 5 checks diagonally. This will involve finding the space between defenders. The ball is then shot first touch at goal.

The 11 rarely receives a pass because of a densely defended goal area, but the 11 checks two or three quick steps from the back post to any perceived opening in front of him. A more likely way to encounter the ball is to be ready to poach off a keeper's fumble from a 2 or 5 shot.

Timing

So when do the players check? If they move too soon, or too late it's a wasted opportunity. Our players check when the 7 has stilled the ball *and* looked up. These two actions lead to our decisive checks.

Weight

The 7 in the above scenario will provide a "medium" pass to the 2. A "firm" pass to the 5. And a "blast" to the 11.

Why the different weights? There are no defenders to pass through for a pass to the 2 because of defender distance rules. A pass to the 5 requires the ball be squeezed between defenders, so a firmer pass is crucial. The pass to the 11 needs to be threaded between multiple defenders and the opposing keeper, so a hard pass is essential.

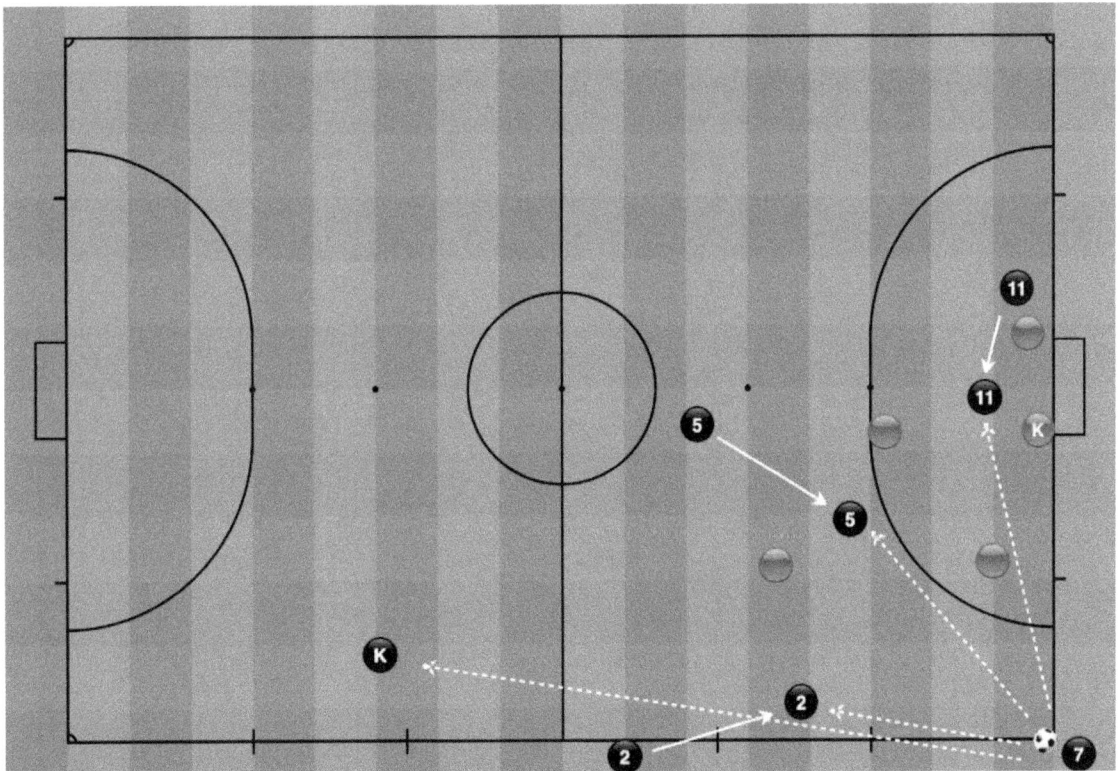

CORNER KICK OPTIONS

Set Plays – into the imagination's labyrinth

> *Free Kicks, Kick-ins, Corners, Clever Keeper*

"Think left and think right and think low and think high. Oh the things you can thinks up if only you try!" – Dr. Seuss

In the movie classic, *Pan's Labyrinth*, the maze provides an unexpected twist at the film's end. A suspicious character suddenly reveals itself as noble. The filmmaker sets a trap, and we fall head first into it. Such slight of hand also plays well with Set Plays. Movement, misdirection, and decoys become the supporting cast to the main actor: the scored goal. It all starts with paper, pencil, and a plan. Scribble and score.

Free Kicks

In the 2012 FIFA Futsal World Cup in Thailand, Spain used this well constructed free kick to score. The 11 sealing the wall with a block is crucial to its success. Miguelin's (2) initial shot did not go in, but Torres (7) poached the rebound to make it 1-1.

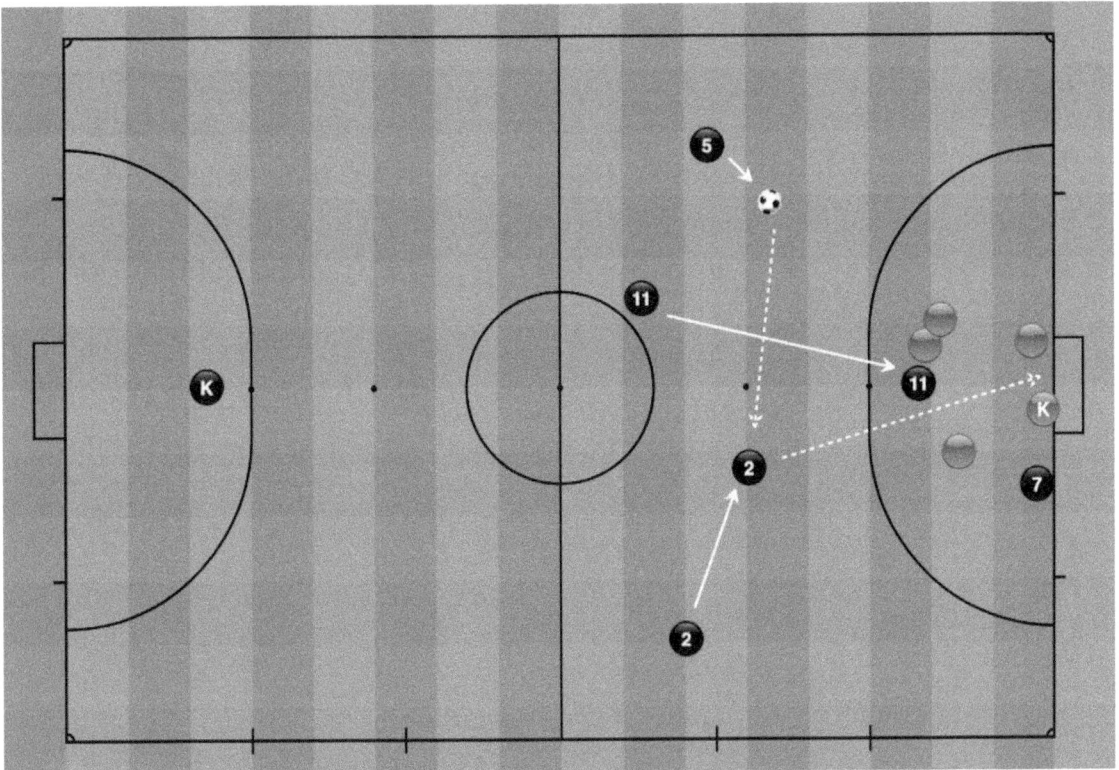

SPAIN vs. BRAZIL – 2012 THAILAND

Kick-ins

In this youth match between FC Barcelona and UD las Rozas Boadilla, UD loops the 7 while the diagonal running 5 & 11 scatter the defense wide. The 7 scores on an uncontested shot. The timing is impeccable as all players start their runs simultaneously.

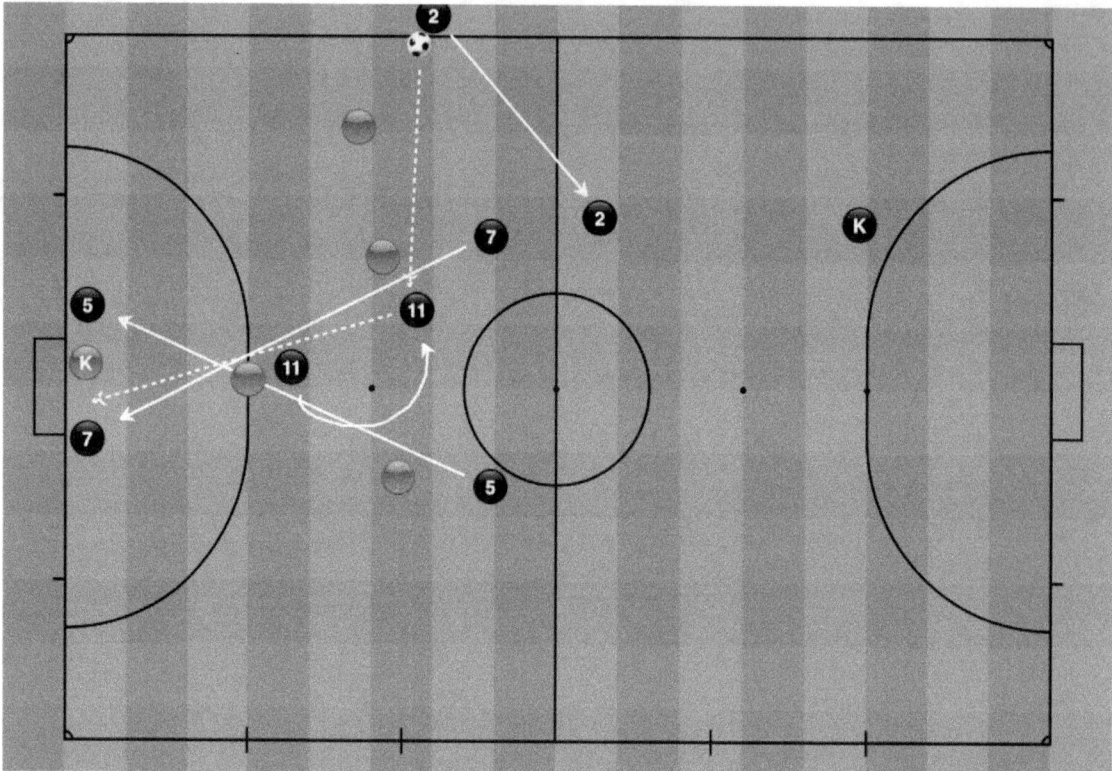

FC Barcelona vs. UD las Rozas Boadilla – X Copa of Spain 2013

Corners

In this set piece the defense loses sight of the 5 when the 7 & 2 combine. The 7 deftly rolls the ball back to the 2 with the sole. The defense is then drawn forward, and the 5 is left free to one time on goal. Along with counter attacks an abundance of goals are found in set plays.

FC BARCELONA vs. INTER MOVISTAR – LNFS 2015

Even keepers can get into the act. Eventual champion Dinamo Moscow opens the middle with this well designed play at the Intercontinental Cup held in Greensboro, North Carolina hosted by USA Futsal.

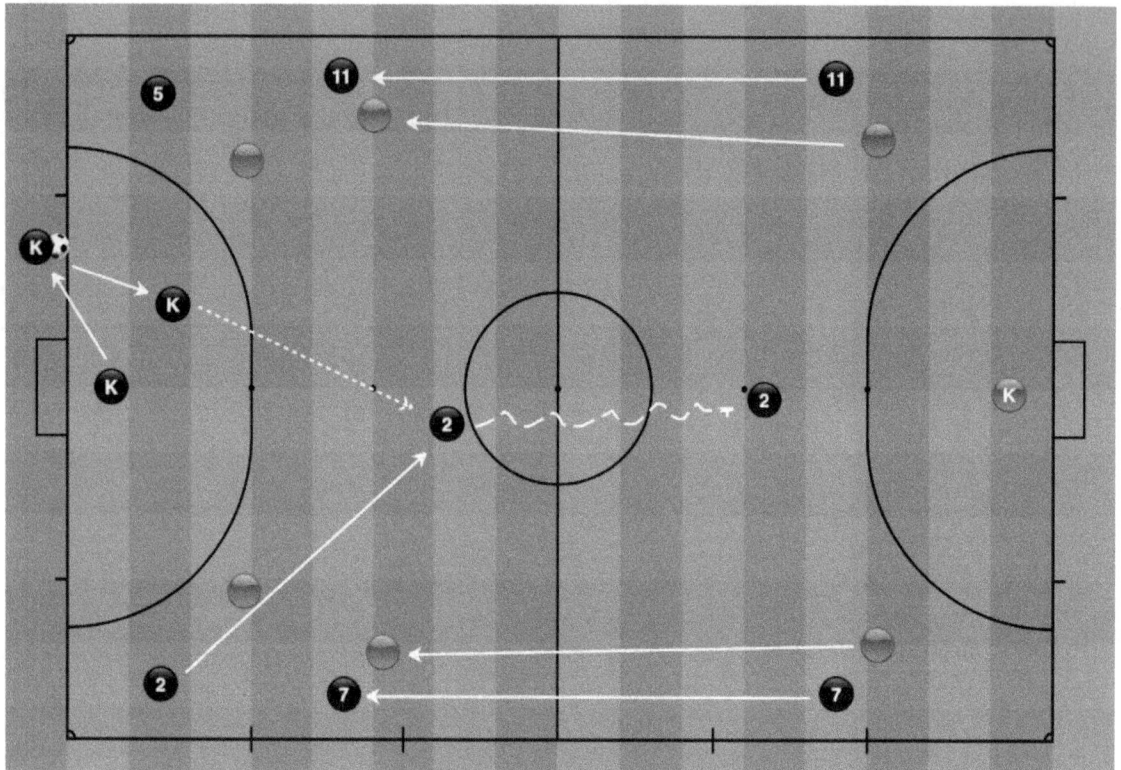

**DINAMO MOSCOW vs. INTELLI/ORLANDIA –
INTERCONTINENTAL CUP 2013**

Defense - half, three quarters, or full court?

> ➤ *Windshield-Whiskers or Four Whiskers*

"Hence that general is skillful in defense whose opponent does not know what to attack." – Sun Tzu

Half - awaiting the opponent in one's own half with two players up and two back forms a "box". This defense is rarely used, but the idea is to limit the area one needs to defend. Defending half a court is easier and more effective than defending a full court, or so the idea goes.

Three Quarters - again lined up with 2 players up and 2 back, this "box" defense enables our *Windshield-Whisker* set up. The 7 & 11 "forwards" play a *pressure-coverage* defense much like the 6 & 8 play in soccer. Ideally the *pressure* defender is able to funnel the opponent to the touchline. In the event our pressure defender is beaten to the middle our *coverage* defender awaits. The back and forth motion mimics that of a windshield wiper and provides a graspable image for our younger players.

The 2 & 5 defenders play *"whisker"* or man-to-man defense. They are to have their arm or "whisker" on the opponent. This ensures they are *one step away* from the passing lane and thus able to *step in front* and intercept.

Full Court - as players grow more adept at close man marking, our *four whiskers* full court press comes into play. This is the ideal defense for putting opponents back on their heels. Our defense is now *dictating* to the opponent. Turnovers in the opponent's half are plentiful and easy goals abound, but only if all *four whiskers* are intensely marking. All defenders are goal side and a step away from the passing lane. Our whisker mantra of *"Nobody in back of you,"* is always in effect. Follow all runners and stay goal side at all times.

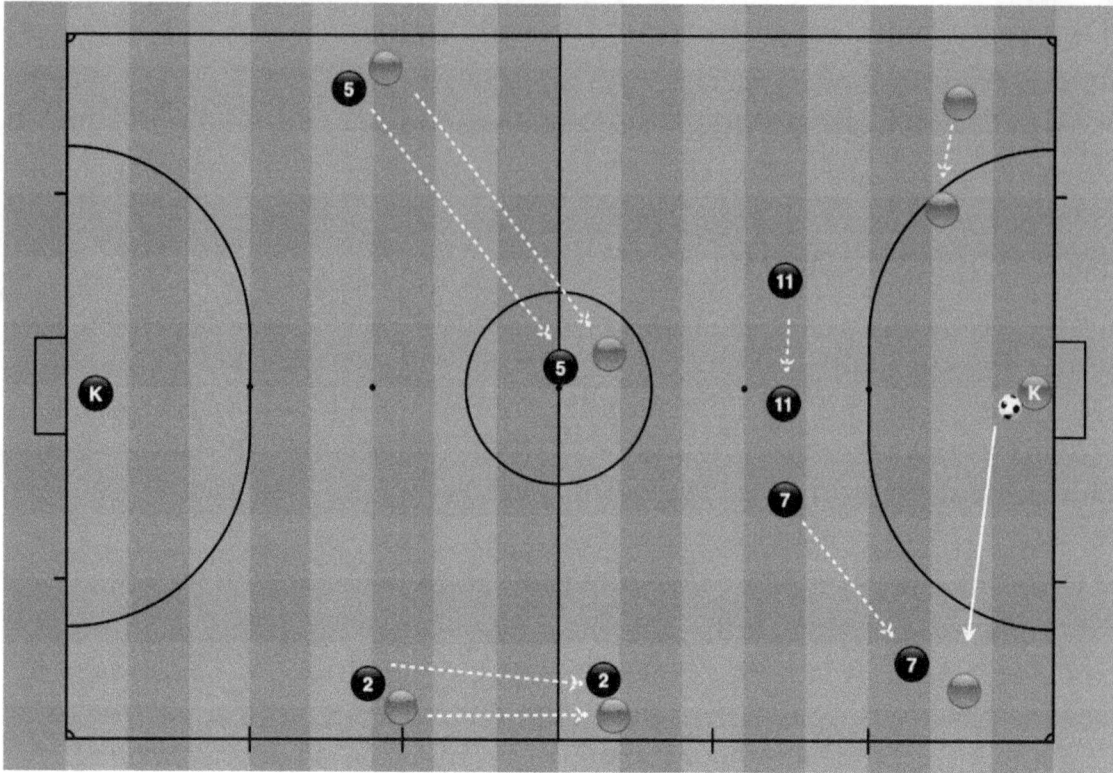

THREE QUARTERS WINDSHIELD-WHISKERS

Defense, Corners – plugging the middle

➤ *Triangle & 1*

"Geometry is not true, it's advantageous." – Henri Poincare

The Triangle is a *zone* meant to deter a pass in front of goal. The 1 is a man-to-man "whisker" behind the zone in the back post area. If the ball is in the corner nearest our 2 position, then the triangle is formed by having our 2 standing on the end line 5 yards away from the ball, the 7 position stands five yards directly in front of the 2, and the 11 is tucked in to form a triangle with each side being roughly equal in length: an equilateral triangle for you geometry buffs. Again this zone is meant to deter any runs into the area in front of goal.

By official rules all defenders must be 5 meters from the ball, so this often allows an "exit alley" along the touchline. If the opponent plays the ball down this alley, our 7 position in the above scenario immediately charges out to deny a shot on goal.

The 2 positions will often kneel and stretch their back leg as far back as possible to deter a pass or shot directly on goal.

The 11's position, the top point of the triangle known as the *"top of the roof,"* is constantly swiveling their head looking for a runner. If an opponent does make a run in front of goal, the 11 is expected to challenge it. The 11 is expected to win all balls played to runners.

The 5 is expected to play goal side defense and deny any poaching attempts by opponents after a shot on goal.

CORNER KICK DEFENSE: TRIANGLE & 1

Defense, Kick-ins – collapsing the middle

> ➤ *4 behind the line of the ball*

"What lies behind you and what lies in front of you, pales in comparison to what lies inside of you." – Ralph Waldo Emerson

Like in soccer, we want to "Get Big" and stretch the opponent when in possession and collapse or "Get Small" when on defense. As a general rule, we do not want our opponent to possess the ball in the middle of the court. An opponent with the ball in the middle simply has too many attacking options.

To lessen the opponent's ability to play into the middle from a kick-in, we have our 2 & 5 play *"whisker"* defense while our 7 stands diagonal from the ball to block the middle. The 11 then tucks in behind the 7 to not allow a split pass and our middle is now secured. All four defenders are behind the line of the ball. The line of the ball is the imaginary line that extends from the ball to the same spot on the opposite sideline. The opponent is then forced to play negative (back).

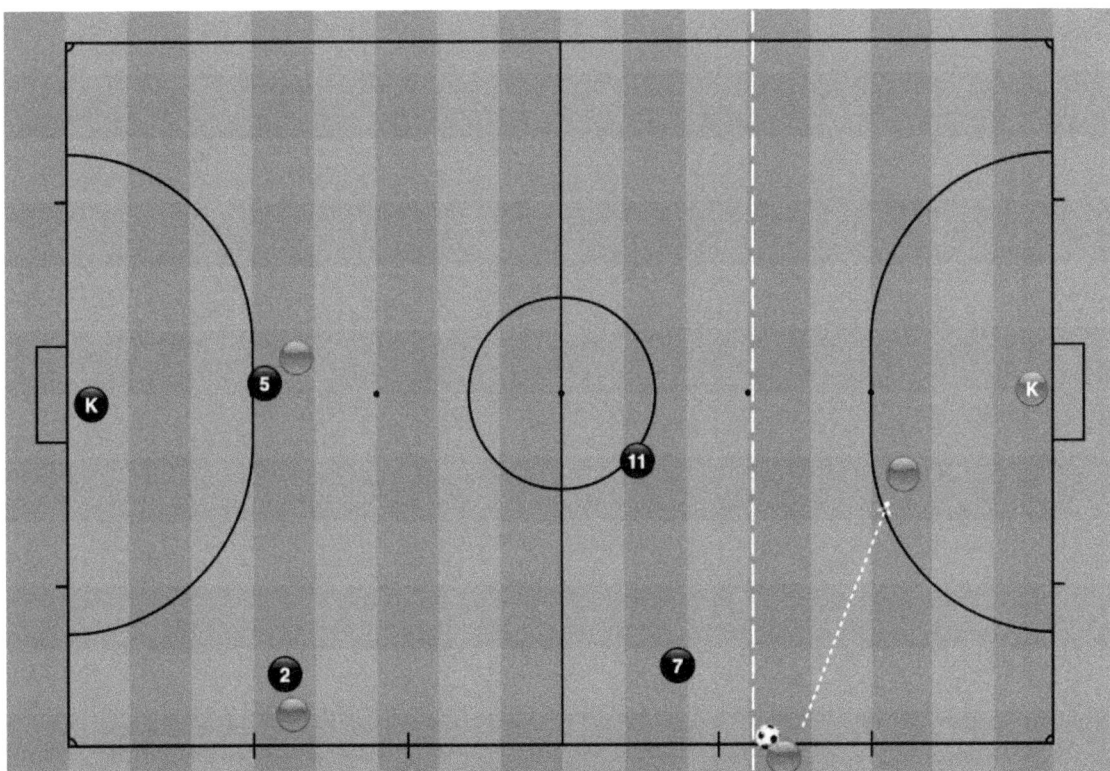

4 BEHIND THE LINE OF THE BALL

Time-Outs – when to use them?

> ➤ *Set plays, momentum breakers, timely rest*

"Time is the wisest counselor of all." – Pericles

Like in basketball or Mexico v Netherlands at Brazil 2014 (LVG, you tricky devil!), time-outs are an option in futsal: one per half. *So when and why do you use them?* A lot of it comes down to personal preference.

Some coaches prefer to save them for *free kicks* to design plays. Others prefer to use them as *momentum breakers* if their team is on the back foot. Also if a team has limited or no subs, the time-out can be used as a *resting and water break* opportunity. Whatever the motivation for using them, they are a golden 60 seconds and should be a vital part of your toolbox.

How to Structure a Training – touches, movements, ideas

"An organization's ability to learn, and translate that learning into action rapidly, is the ultimate competitive advantage." – Jack Welch

Futsal training minutes are precious, rare, and often wasted. Warm ups without the ball, long lines, and random drills that do not serve your system of play are all enemies to maximizing your minutes. After our training sessions the kids are free to whoop it up and heave three point shots at the basketball stands where we train. But during training, the focus and group attitude must be professional. There must be an *urgency* to trainings. We don't believe in off days. Every player and every coach will bring 100% effort. No excuses.

Ok, let me get off my soapbox without tripping over a bag of balls. Our training ideas are filtered through:

1) Ball Mastery
2) Checking
3) Dribbling - 1v1
4) Passing - Movement & Multiple Touches
5) Passing - Decision Making
6) Tactical Awareness

Almost every training session includes drills from *Ball Mastery, Dribbling-1v1,* and *Passing-Decision Making.* They are considered essential areas of development. Checking, Passing-Movement & Multiple Touches, and Tactical Awareness are mixed in. These training areas are not exclusive and often overlap. We normally run through four drills before going to scrimmage. Scrimmages are frequently stopped until players learn positioning especially from kick-ins and throw-ins.

We are firm believers that *less is more.* So our players master a limited number of drills. There are enough drills to provide variety, but not too many to dilute mastery. The following exercises are staples of our program.

Ball Mastery

How often have we heard American players are not technical enough? It is an identified weakness going back decades. Identified weaknesses need to be remedied. So every training starts with a Ball Mastery drill. Dribble Boxes is a favorite.

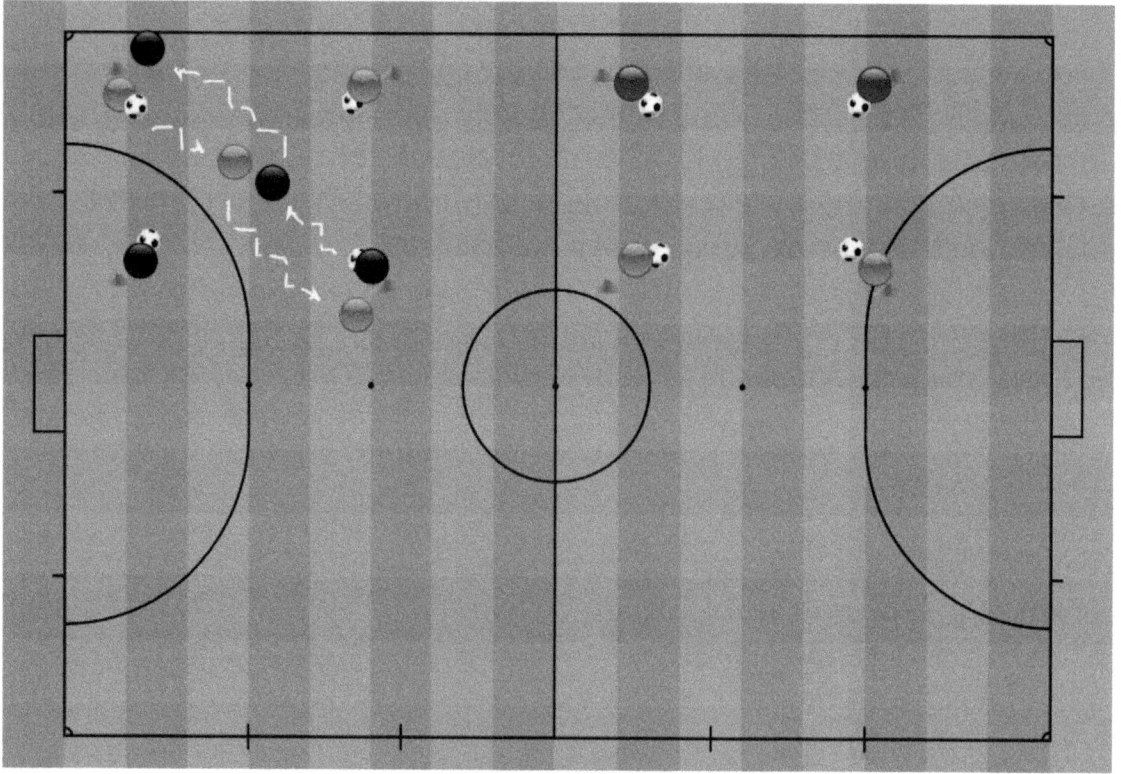

DRIBBLE BOXES

Set up:
- 1 player per cone
- 1 ball per player
- 7 x 7 yard grid

Instructions:
1. Players dribble diagonally at each other.
2. Players execute move in front of each other.
3. Players dribble with light touches to opposite side.
4) Repeat with other diagonal members of grid.

These dribbles are our focus, but many others can be applied:
1) Sole-control
2) Iniesta
3) Drag/push-out
4) Dime stop

Variation:
- Players complete dribble and then using the sole, drag-turn back to original cone

Coaching points:
1) Head up
2) Light touches
3) Accelerate out of move
4) Train with both feet

Checking

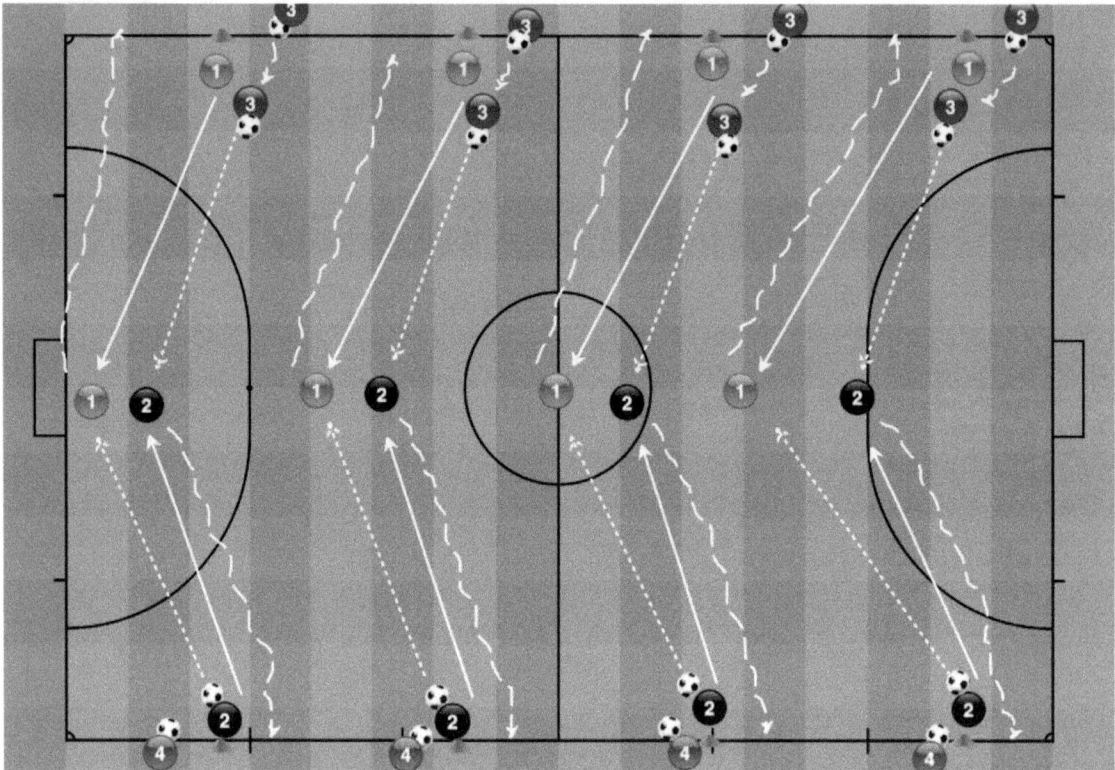

DIAGONAL CHECKS

Set up:
- 4 players per checking lane
- 3 balls
- 2 markers per lane

Instructions:
1) All 1's check diagonal in same direction
2) Player 2 times pass to arrive at midcourt
3) Player 1 receives with the sole of outside foot and then drag-turns and dribbles back to the marker.
4) Repeat with player 2 now checking and player 3 passing.

Variations:
- Checker dribbles ball back with specific move, (sole roll, sole-control, Iniesta, etc.)

- Checker takes two steps away before checking while player on the ball fakes pass to side (misdirection) and then passes

Coaching Points:
1) Check hard
2) Call for ball
3) Checker turns in the direction that ball is dragged
4) Dribble back quickly and with light touches

Dribbling - 1v1

FOUR SECOND DRIBBLE

Set up:
- 5-6 players
- 3 balls
- Half court

Instructions:
1) Player 1 passes firmly to player 2.
2) Player 2 has four seconds to dribble past player 1 with specific coach requested dribble.
3) Player 2 is a cooperative, passive defender and will not take the ball.
4) Player 2 can only shoot after dribbling past player 1.
5) Players 1 and 2 switch lines with 2 retrieving the ball.

Variation:
- Player 1 uses dribble of choice, and player 2 becomes aggressive, active defender and looks to take the ball

Coaching Points:
1) Count four seconds aloud to create urgency
2) Encourage all creative moves even if not successful
3) Point out defender basics of stopping dribbler's forward progress, guiding to weaker foot, and stepping between dribbler and ball after heavy touch

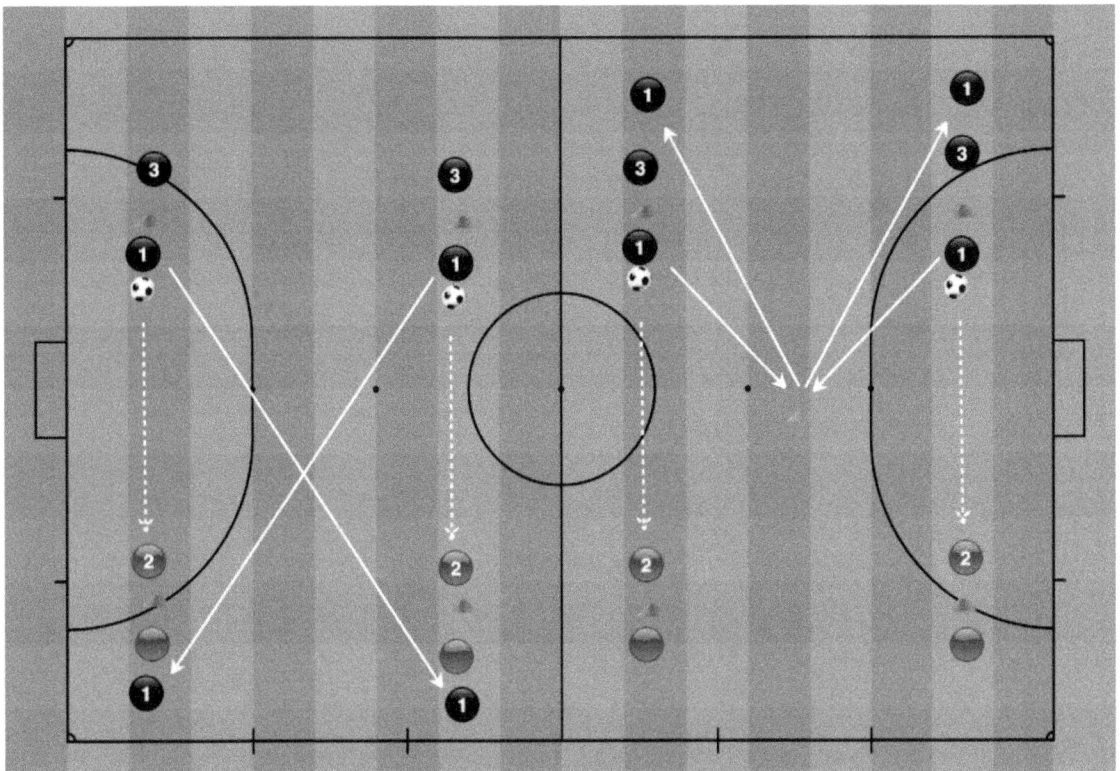

"PASS STRAIGHT, RUN DIAGONAL"

Set up:
- 8 players
- 2 balls
- 8 x 10 yard grid

Instructions:
1) Left image: players 1 pass forward then run diagonal to cone, and then returns to the same line. Players 2 repeat on opposite side.
2) Right image: Players 1 pass straight and run diagonal to opposite side. Players 2 repeat pattern.

Variations:
- Left side image: pass straight, run diagonal, and continue to line directly in front
- Right side image: pass diagonal and run straight
- Attempt one touch on quality passes

Coaching points:
1) Roll ball forward to be able to step into the ball for increased power and accuracy.
2) Kick the middle of the ball to keep it rolling flat on the surface. This makes the ball easier to receive.
3) Receive the ball with the sole of the foot.
4) Have players say the mantra "Sole-roll-pop!" during the first minute.
5) Have players call out name of passer before receiving.
6) Point out this pattern replicates the 2-7 or 5-11 wall pass.

Passing - Decision Making

These drills usually have some element of Rondo or Keep Away to them. Quick passing decisions to maintain possession are the key. One or two touch passing is the goal. The following drill promotes early support, passing angles, and quickness of play.

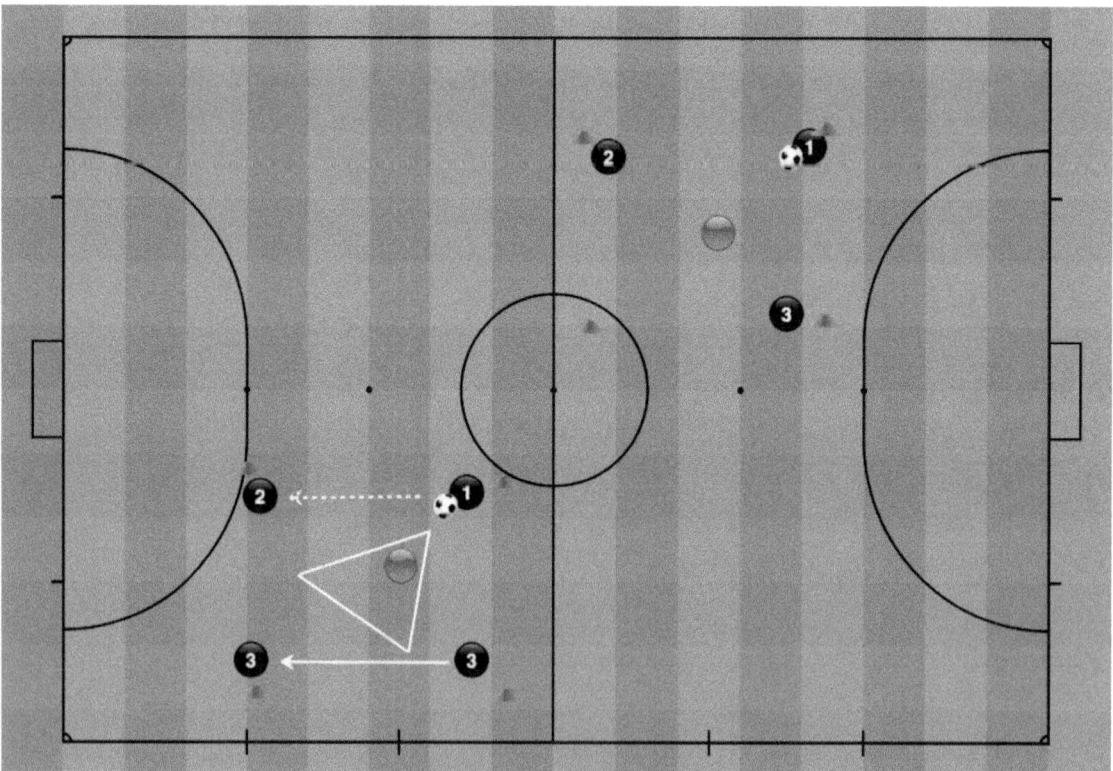

FOUR CORNER SLIDE

Set up:
- 4 players
- 1 ball
- 8 x 8 yard grid

Instructions:
1) Player with ball should always have two passing options.
2) "Monkey in the middle" defender looks to take the ball.
3) Require two touches: one to control and one to pass.
4) Ball can only be played left or right, never diagonal.
5) Here player 1 passes to player 2.
6) Player 3 then rotates to open marker to provide player 2 with two passing options.

Variations:
- Require one touch passing when possible, (quality pass)
- At younger ages, "monkey" may be cooperative and passively chase ball to increase possession

Coaching points:
1) Insist that 3rd player run to the marker to create best passing angle.
2) Hit middle of the ball to keep it flat on the surface.
3) Insist on player communication, "hey, yeah-yeah, ball, or name".

Tactical Awareness

Drills that replicate an actual game pattern are priceless. In the Triple Wall Pass, we maintain possession and build from the back. The pattern is now second nature for our players and appears frequently in games.

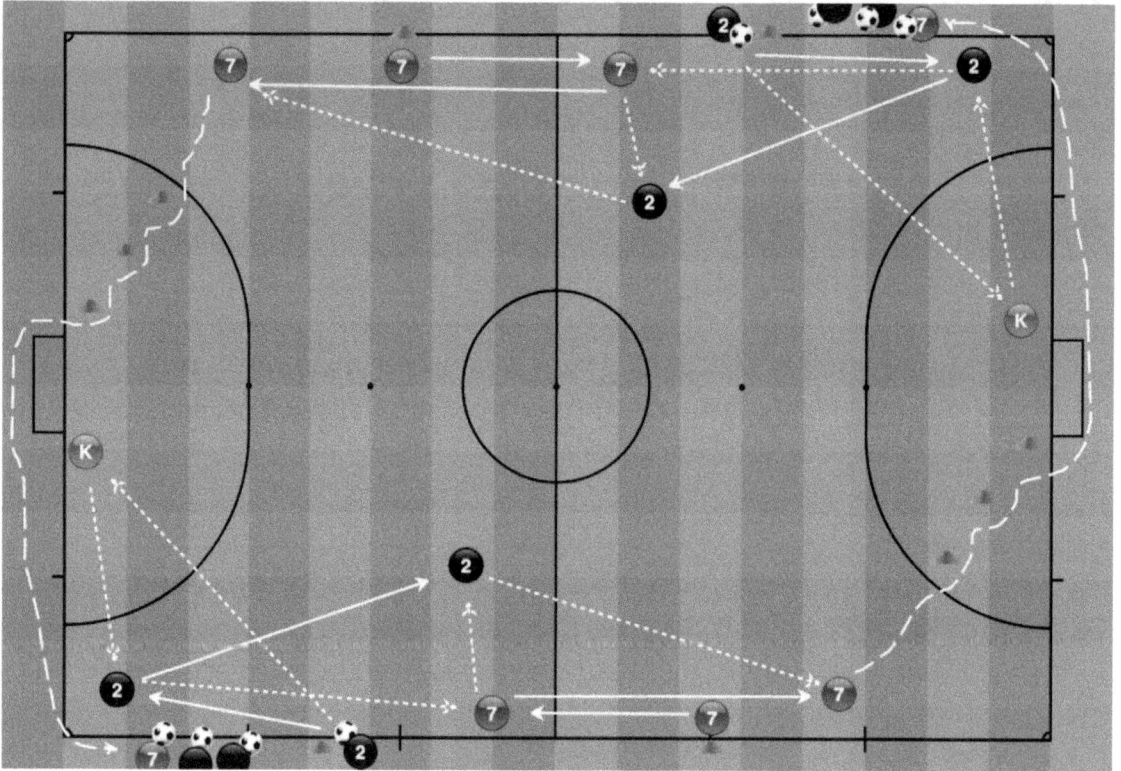

TRIPLE WALL PASS

Set up:
- 8-10 players
- 6-8 balls
- 10 flat markers

Instructions:
1) The 2 position plays the Keeper and checks down the sideline.
2) The Keeper plays the 2 back.
3) The 2 plays the checking 7.
4) The 7 plays the 2 back.
5) The 7 runs up the line and receives the ball.
6) The 7 dribbles through the markers and goes to the opposite side.
7) The 2 takes the starting spot of the 7 position and the pattern repeats.

Variation:
- 1 touch passing

Coaching points:
1) The 2 looks up-court while kicking-in and then looks back and plays the Keeper. This will keep a defense from cheating forward.
2) Hit the middle of the ball to keep it flat on the surface and make the passes more receivable.
3) Checks are hard and timely.
4) No lead passes, instead pass to feet.

Final Thoughts – a journey worth taking

"The only journey is the one within." – Rainer Maria Rilke

Winning Futsal is really about attractive, attacking play. Even our defense is an extension of our offense. If we're faithful to our ideas and train with focus, then winning becomes a byproduct. Winning, though, is never the goal. We seek to develop players to their fullest. Team wise, we look to create as many scoring opportunities as possible while preventing as many as possible. It's that simple. Along those lines, we rotate players evenly on the "forward" and "defensive" lines, provide for equal playing time, and we shake the refs hand after each game. Equality, fairness, and sportsmanship make for *Winning Futsal*. Futsal is just a tool to better our kids' lives and perhaps our own.

Good luck on your journey!

Rob Bell
BUSC Director of Futsal
www.bulldogsfutsal.com

Note:
The Winning Futsal series will soon publish a book and video that elaborate on our program, training drills, and system of play. Stay tuned!

www.ingramcontent.com/pod-product-compliance
Lightning Source LLC
LaVergne TN
LVHW080054090426
835513LV00031B/1235